D1379638

Origami: Rokoan Style

The Art of Connecting Cranes

Masako Sakai – Michie Sahara

Heian

©1998 Masako Sakai-Michie Sahara
Edited by Dianne Ooka
Photograph: Don Farber
Diagram Illustration and Typography: Ashley B. Lang

First Edition 1998
98 99 00 01 02 03 04 05 9 8 7 6 5 4 3 2 1

ISBN: 0-89346-875-4

HEIAN International, Inc.
1815 W. 205th Street, Suite #301
Torrance, CA 90501
E-mai: Heianemail@heian.com
Website: www.Heian.com

Printed in Singapore

Table of Contents

Part 1:

Introduction to Rokoan Tsunagiori Style

    Who is Rokoan?
    Type of paper you can use
    How to fold an Origami Crane the Traditional Way
    A quick and easy way to fold a crane
    Basic Folds & Symbols

Part 2:

Instructions on models created by Rokoan

Part 3:

How to display your finished Origami work.

Part 1:
Introduction to Rokoan Tsunagiori Style
Who is Rokoan?
What is Rokoan Origami Style?

Today the art of paper folding is enjoyed throughout the world. While forms of paper folding traditions exist in different cultures internationally, the strongest tradition comes from Japan. Because of this, many countries have adopted the Japanese word ORIGAMI and use it to mean paper folding.

The word ORIGAMI is made up of two words: ORI, meaning "to fold" and Kami or Gami, meaning "paper".

People usually fold animals, flowers, birds, singly. But the ORIGAMI we are introducing here is called Rokoan Tsunagiori Style Origami. With this style of ORIGAMI, you fold multiple number of connected cranes all out of a single sheet of paper that is cut into a series of connecting squares. The word TSUNAGIORI is made up of two Japanese words: TSUNAGI meaning "connecting" and ORI meaning "to fold".

This style of folding was created by Rokoan Gido (1761-1834), a Buddhist priest. He was the third son of the tenth chief priest of Choenji temple in the Kuwana (Castle) district of Mie Prefecture. Rokoan himself became the eleventh chief priest of this temple. His writings and research papers on the Kuwana district are stored at the Kuwana City National Treasure. He did not write much about himself in these papers, but, according to a book called "ORITSURU-KI" (Crane folding Journal) by Hirose Mosai, Rokoan took 18 years perfecting his style of ORIGAMI. In his book, Mosai praised Rokoan highly, saying, "Rokoan's style of origami was not only enjoyed by children and women. One has created such versatile origami.... making ten, even hundreds of cranes appear out of one sheet of paper. Such a fabulous art has never been accomplished!" Rokoan compiled 49 models he created with this style into a book called "Senbatsuru Orikata" (Folding a Thousand Cranes). This is considered the oldest book on origami.

Each model had its own title and its own poem written by Akisato Ritoh, a famous poet and a writer of several travel books of the time. Up to 100 connected cranes are folded using this method. Unlike other ORIGAMI, you do use scissors, but no glue is used to connect the cranes. It is all in the pattern.... areas you cut and areas you leave uncut.

According to Mosai who has studied Rokoan's journals, there should be another book written by Rokoan, called "SOUNKAKU" (Fundamental Cranes in the Cloud). It featured one hundred models of five hundred cranes in different positions. This was to be the follow up to the first book. However, this book has never been found anywhere.

The poems written by Akisato Ritoh used puns on words that were current in those days. Sometimes he used a part of a popular poem; at other times he satirized poems. It is thought that Ritoh named each model. He was totally overwhelmed by Rokoan's talent, and felt that Rokoan had created beautiful art, not just play for children and women. He befriended Rokoan and learned to fold several models. Some historians say that Ritoh compiled the book "Senbatsuru Orikata", but Jun Hiraoka, now deceased head of Kuwana City Cultural Museum, certified that it is written by Rokoan, according to journals of the time.

Rokoan's "Senbatsuru Orikata" was printed and reprinted by five publishers in Osaka, Kyoto and Edo (Tokyo). For an origami book it was published extensively. Yet his style of origami did not catch on until twenty or thirty years ago. Why? One reason is that Rokoan's origami is difficult to fold and also difficult to explain. Another reason might be that the artists who drew the pictures and diagrams and the artisans who carved the woodblocks for printing, did not understand themselves what they were creating. Thus, only the easiest origami models became popular.

Fascinated by Rokoan's book, my mother, Masako Sakai, recreated all 49 models on her own. Using this style, she has created her own models called "Noren", a room divider, and "Tsuru Furin", crane wind chime. In this book we have selected models with diverse designs. We have put them in a slightly different sequence than Rokoan's. The models gradually become more difficult to fold, so we suggest that you just be patient and enjoy folding.

Type of paper you can use

To fold Rokoan Style Origami we need paper that is fairly thin but strong since the connection between cranes is as small as one-eigth of an inch. "Washi", Japanese paper, is used. It is very strong because it is made out of fibers from barks of trees such as KOZO, GAMPI or MITSUMATA which are part of the mulberry family. Washi can come in plain white form, but many different finished forms of washi are sold. Washi is usually sold by a sheet. Each sheet is approximately 24" x 36". You must cut this into the size for your model. In doing this make sure that the square you cut is as perfect as possible. This will affect your folding. Here is a list of washi that you can use to fold Rokoan Style Origami.

Mingeishi:
Plain solid color washi. It is the cheapest washi, and great for beginners or for practice. Smooth side is the right side.

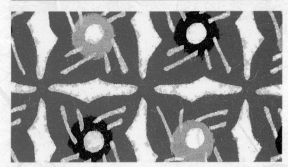

Jo-washi:
Washi with design, but normally no gold tone is used. Very strong. Good for models with numerous connections such as #25 TSURIFUNE.

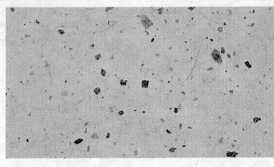

Chiri-zome:
Solid color with speckles. Thin and strong. Great for models where you have several layers of paper to fold a single crane. Smooth side is the right side.

Ita jime:
White washi with one color dye. Thin and strong. Good for models that show both sides of the paper. Smooth side is the right side.

Yuzenshi

Washi with colorful Yuzen designs like a kimono. Strong but thick because of layers of paint. The finished models are beautiful, but certain models cannot be made with this because the paper is too thick. With this paper, the part of the paper, which is usually folded into cranes, can be cut off. (You will understand what we mean once you start to fold.)

Mino-gami:

Plain white washi. Very strong and thin, but really good quality is very expensive.

Bokashi-zome kinko:

White washi with dye that looks like clouds with gold or silver speckles. Usually one color, sometimes several. Good for models where thin paper is required and where both sides of the paper are shown.

Double-sided washi:

One side is gold or silver and the other side is a solid color. This is great for two-toned. #4 Imoseyama.

Taiwan Yuzen:

Designs are somewhat similar to Japanese Yuzen. Less refined than Japanese Yuzen, but quite strong washi paper.

7

How to fold an Origami crane....
The Traditional way

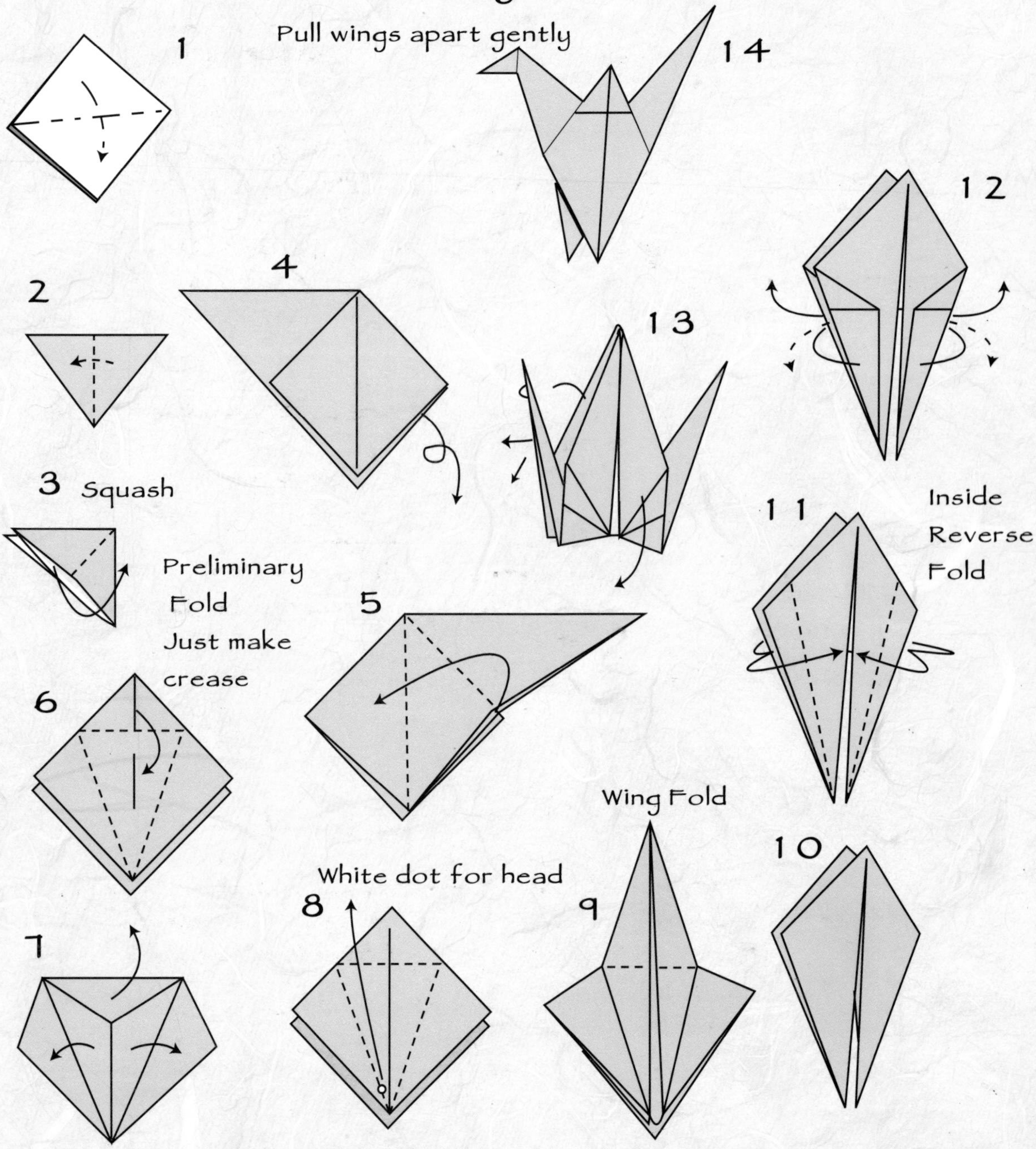

1

Pull wings apart gently

14

2

4

13

12

3 Squash

Preliminary
Fold
Just make
crease

5

11 Inside
Reverse
Fold

6

Wing Fold

8 White dot for head

9

10

7

Lift upper layer only.
Press it down on crosswise crease.
Edges roll inward and meet.

A Quick and Easy way to fold a crane:

The traditional way of folding a crane is illustrated on the previous page. With our Rokoan Style Origami, it helps to know how to fold a crane as easily as possible since you are folding multiple cranes all connected at the head, tail and wings. The following short cut allows you to get to step #10 of traditional crane folding very quickly.

1.   Make a vertical crease, a horizontal crease and diagonal creases. All creases are the Mountain Fold except one of the diagonal creases (which is going to represent a head and a tail) which is a Valley Fold. Be sure to do the vertical and horizontal creases firmly. This will help you later when you want the back of the crane to go up when you do the following move in #3.

2.   Fold corner B to line A-C making crease A-b; fold corner D to line A-C making crease A-d; do the same to all corners. When folding multiple cranes, you make these creases to all the cranes before you start folding each crane. It might seem like you are folding more, but this is better in the long run. First it gives you more precise creases than doing the traditional #6 fold. Second, it is easier to get to #10 than folding the traditional folds #8 and #9.

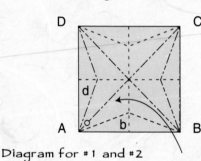

Diagram for #1 and #2

This is the only Valley Fold.

The rest are all Mountain Folds.

3.   All corners (A through D) of your origami crane paper represent head, tail or wings. With the Rokoan Origami Style, we designate the head by marking it with a little white dot. Since A is marked as the head, C is the tail; B and D therefore are wings. Fold diagonal crease A-C as the Valley Fold and bring A to meet C.

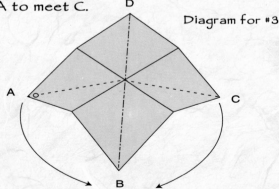

Diagram for #3

4.   Lift wings B and D up. Now you are at step #10 of the traditional
     crane fold.

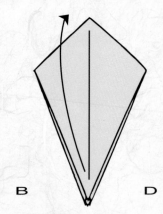

Diagram for #4

5.   At step #11 of the traditional crane fold, you fold to the center.
     With our style, however you fold about 2/3 of the way, leaving
     about 1/3 of the space from the center. This makes the head and
     tail neater. Since washi is thicker than regular origami paper,
     folding it in the traditional way makes the head look too bulky
     -- like a dinosaur's head.

Leave about 1/3 space from the center.

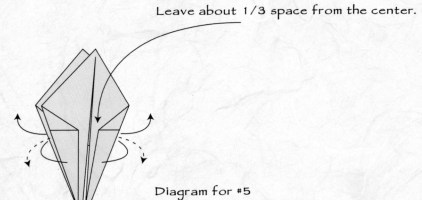

Diagram for #5

Tips for Rokoan Origami Style Folding:

1. Regardless of which model you are folding, do not forget to make all the creases at the beginning before you fold an individual crane. Even a difficult model can be folded with ease when all the creases are made ahead.

2. Before you fold, mark each head with a white dot on the right side of your paper. When folding multiple numbers of cranes, marking heads is the only way for you to know where all the heads are. A black dot is used to mark a head that is to match another head with a white dot. This is done when two sheets of paper are folded to make one crane. Usually the right side of the paper marked with a black dot is placed under the wrong side of the paper with the white dot marked on its right side. The only time this is not followed is with #25 Tsurifune.

3. Remember that the head is where you make the Valley Fold. This means that the opposite of the head, the tail, is also done with the Valley Fold.

4. The connection between the cranes, which you leave uncut, is approximately 1/8".

5. Areas marked with triangles are unused portions. This area is to be included into a crane. Each instruction will tell you into which crane you should include it. Rokoan's original instruction states it this way. We feel you should be able to fold layers of Mingeishi, Itajime, Chiri-zome and Jo-washi, but it is very difficutl to fold layers of Yuzenshi since it is thick with colorful paints. You should cut off the area marked with a triangle (unused portion) in order to fold smoothly. In Rokoan's time it is believed that only white washi was available. So this was not a problem.

6. The models in this book should be completed in their sequence of presentation, since they become progressively difficult.

If you pay attention to the above points you can fold all models with ease.

Basic Folds and Symbols

Valley Fold — — — — — — — — — — — — —

Mountain Fold — · — · — · — · — · — · — ·

Existing Crease ————————————————

Direction to Fold →——————————————→

Zabuton Ori or
Blintz Fold

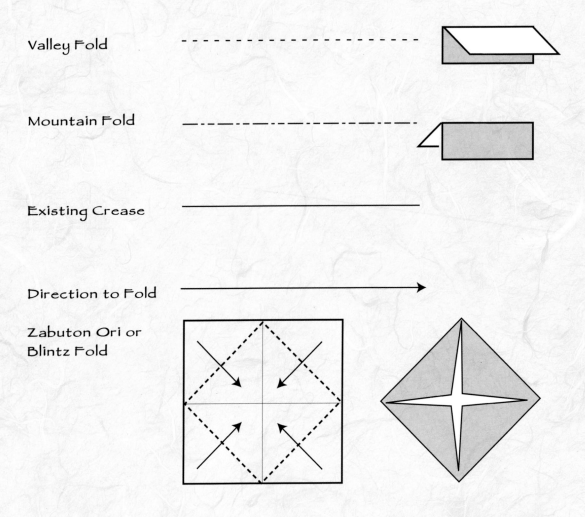

Shaded area is the
right side of the paper

Part 2

1. Ehiroi..... Feeding Time

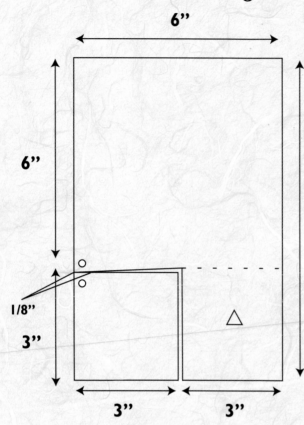

6"

6"

9"

1/8"

3"

3"   3"

This is a cute model of a mother crane feeding her baby. It is the easiest of Rokoan Origami Crane Style. The connection between the two is at the heads and is slightly bigger than 1/8 of an inch. Be careful not to cut or tear it.

Note:
Remeber to mark the heads with white dots.
Remeber to make all the creases for folding before you cut. Fold the area marked with a triangle into the adult crane. Fold the adult crane first.

2. Sazanami..... Rippling Waves

This is as easy as Ehiroi. The heads of four cranes are connected at the center by leaving approximately 1/4 inch of the paper uncut.

<u>Note:</u>
Remember to make all the creases for folding before you cut.

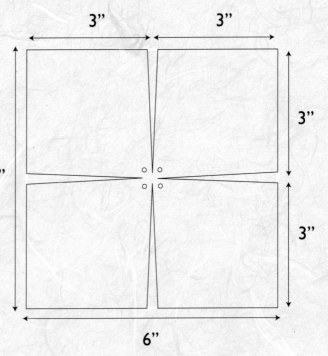

3"   3"

3"

6"

3"

6"

14

3. Hanami Kuruma..... Flower-Viewing Wagon

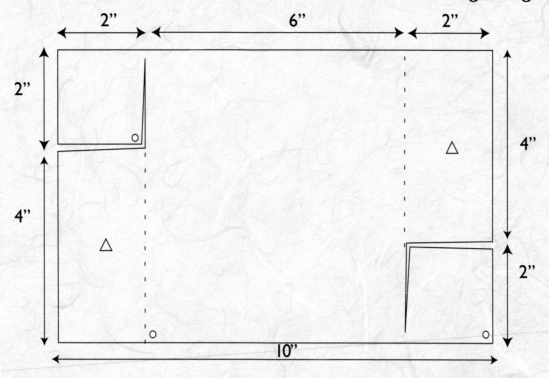

In this model, two two-inch-square baby cranes and one six-inch-square adult crane are connected at their wings.

Note:

Be sure to fold the areas marked with triangles into the six-inch-square adult crane. Remember to mark the heads with white dots. Remember to make all the creases for folding before you cut.

4. Imoseyama..... Imose Mountain

This model is made up of two cranes sharing one body. In Nara Prefecture there are two mountains, Imoyama and Seyama, divided by the Yoshino River. Together these mountains are considered lovers, or a married couple, and are called Imoseyama. This makes a great wedding or anniversary gift.

Note:
Remember to make all the creases for folding before you cut. Remember to mark the heads with white dots. To make a two toned Imoseyama, use reversible washi paper. Fold one crane one color and fold the other crane the other color.

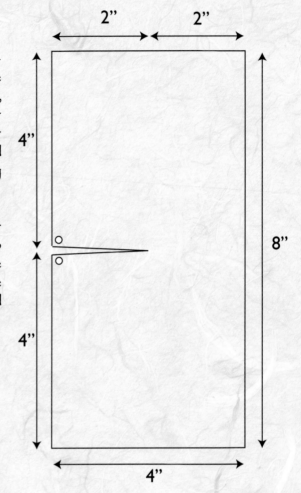

16

5. Yakanbei..... The Fox

This is very similar to #4. Imoseyama, the only difference is that the positions of the heads are at the opposite ends. Please study the diagram carefully.

Simply positioning the two heads differently gives a finished work with a totally different appearance.

<u>Note:</u>

Remember to make all the creases for folding before you cut.

Remember to mark the heads with white dots.

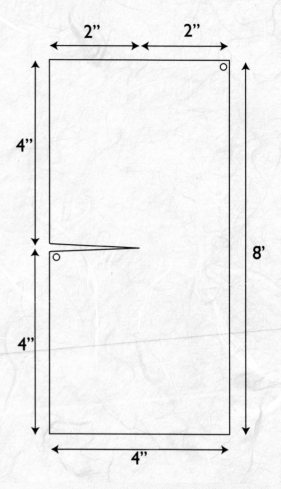

6. Yoshiwara Suzume..... The Sparrows of Yoshiwara

This model is made up of one adult crane in the center with a baby crane at each corner. The areas marked with triangles are folded into the adult crane at the center. The use of thin washi is necessary since the adult crane is made up of three layers of paper.

<u>Note:</u>

There are other models that use this basic idea of one large crane in the center with small cranes attached to it... such as Nuno Sarashi, Hina Asobi, Furan and Tsurifune.

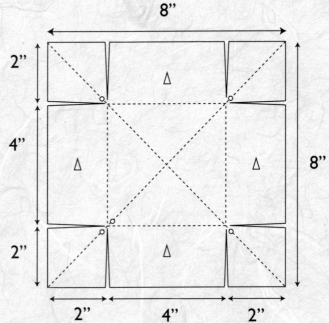

Remember to make all the creases before you fold. Diagonal creases are easier to make before you cut.

1. Asagao..... Morning Glory

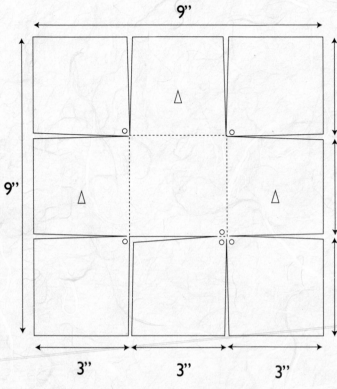

9"

9"

3" 3" 3"

3" 3" 3"

In this model one crane is connected to each corner of the center crane except at one corner, where there are two cranes connected. The areas marked with triangles are folded into the crane in the center just as in #6 Yoshiwara Suzume. Since the center crane must be folded out of four layers of paper, the use of thin washi is once again necessary.

<u>Note:</u>
Remember to make all the creases before you fold.
Remember to mark all the heads.

<u>Tips for presentation:</u>
Since the title of this model is Asagao, Morning Glory, place the small cranes like the petals of a morning glory around the center crane.

8. Nuno Sarashi..... Washing Clothes

In this model three baby cranes are attached to the adult's head and another three baby cranes are attached to the adult's tail.

Note:

Remember to mark all the heads clearly. Remember to make all the creases first. Study the diagram well and use extra care in cutting.

Tips for presentation:

The finished art work can be hung or pasted on a board as a fabulous display.

9. Kumagai..... General Kumagai

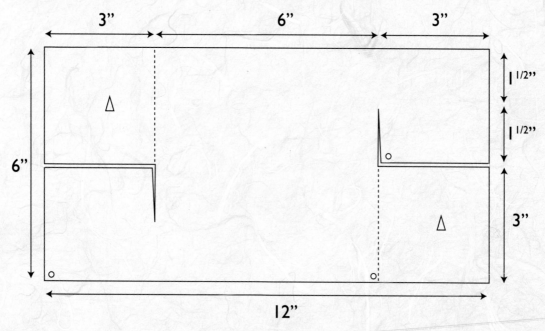

This model consists of an adult crane with two baby cranes attached under the wings... one baby under each wing.

Note:

Remember to fold the area with triangles into the adult crane.

Fold the adult crane first.

Two baby cranes are attached on the back side of the adult's wings.

21

10. Kuretake..... Bamboo

Here two baby cranes are connected between the adult crane's tail and one wing even as they are to each other.

Note:
Remember to mark the heads clearly.
Remember to make all the creases before you fold.

Tips for presentation:
Stylize the finished work by bringing the tail of the adult crane straight up and placing its wings very low as in the picture.

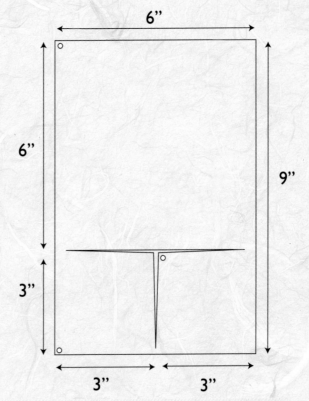

11. Kakitsubata..... The Iris Flower

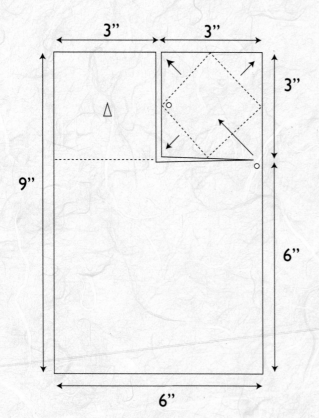

A charming model of an adult crane picking up the baby crane by its back. With this model the adult crane is folded as usual, but the baby crane is folded with the "zabuton ori" or "blintz fold". Whenever you do a "blintz fold" it is necessary to use thin washi.

<u>Note:</u>

The adult crane's head is connected to the baby crane at its back. To achieve this you do a "blintz fold" ... folding one corner close to the adult crane over toward the top center of the baby crane (valley fold) and folding the other three corners under the center of the baby crane (mountain fold). This is a little different from a standard blintz fold (see Basic Folds and Symbols).

12. Murakumo..... The Cloud

In this model the tail of the adult crane is connected to the bottom of the baby crane. The baby crane is folded in "zabuton ori" or "blintz fold".

Note:

Remember to mark all the heads clearly.

Fold the area marked with a triangle into the adult crane.

Remember to make all the creases.

The blintz fold is done in the standard way.

Tips for presentation:

By using a fairly large sheet of washi in gold or silver, the finished work can look quite grand.

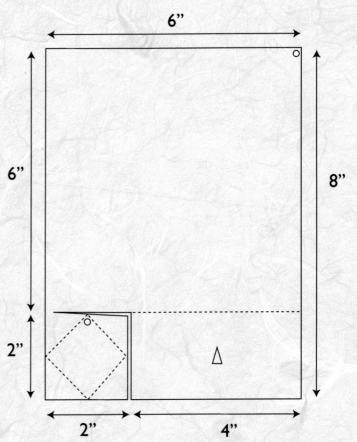

13. Mukashi Otoko..... The Playboy

Two baby cranes are connected to the adult crane at its tail. The adult crane is folded in the "zabuton ori" or "blintz fold" and the two baby cranes are each folded from two sheets of washi. This means that each crane is made up of two layers of paper. The use of thin washi is necessary.

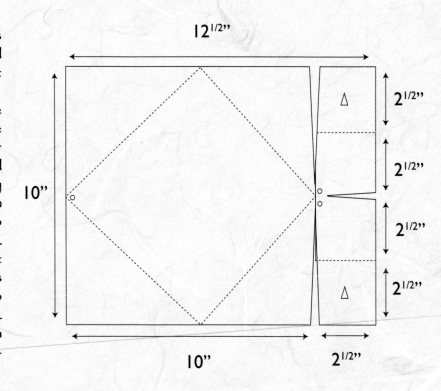

Note:

Remember to mark all the heads clearly and make all the creases before you fold. Fold the areas marked with triangles into the baby cranes.

14. Inazuma..... Lightning

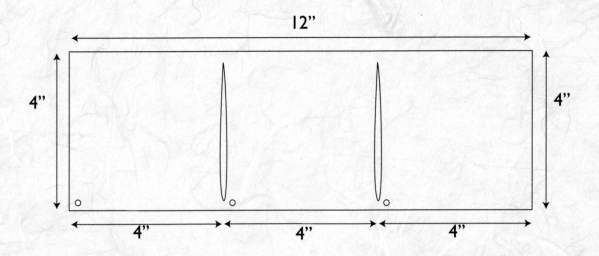

With Inazuma the cranes are connected at two places: a wing to a head and a wing to a tail. This requires you to be more careful with the connections.

<u>Note:</u>
Remember to make all the creases before you fold.
Remember to mark all the heads.

15. Yatsuhashi..... Eight Bridges

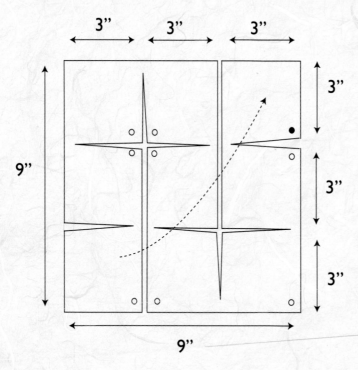

Eight cranes are connected to each other at the wings to form a circle. To make a circle you fold together two end square pieces. You are in fact, folding a single crane out of two square papers. Be sure to match heads with the white and black dots. Do this after you have folded all the other cranes.

Note:
Remember to make all the creases and mark all the heads before you fold.
Have all the heads facing the same direction when you have finished folding.

16. Yottsu No Sode..... Four Sleeves

Four cranes are connected at the wings and two of them connected at the heads also. Take extra care when cutting the paper.

<u>Note:</u>

Remember to make all the creases before you fold.

Remember to mark all the heads.

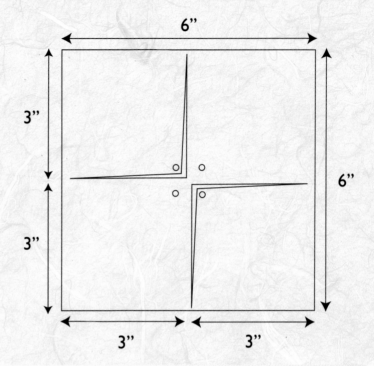

17. Kazaguruma..... The Pinwheel

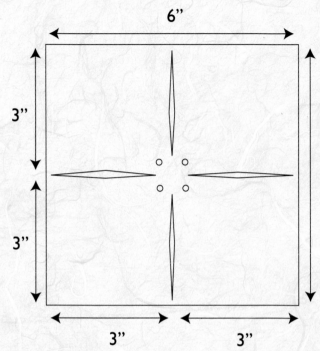

Kazaguruma, a pinwheel, is very similar to the previous model #16 Yottsu No Sode. With this model, however, all the wings and all the heads are connected.

The picture in the original book is drawn like a Japanese family crest, but the finished piece does not look like a crest.

Note:

Remember to make all the creases before you fold.

Remember to mark all the heads.

18. Naruko..... Bird Clapper

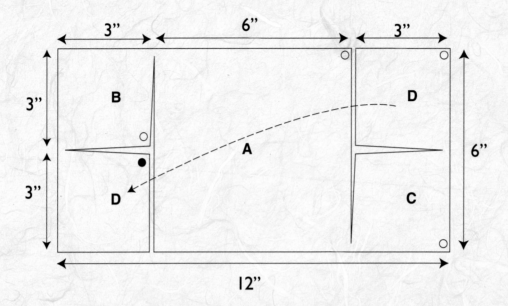

"Naruko" is a Japanese word for a tool used to chase away birds in a rice paddy. It is made up of rows of bamboo sticks on a board with a string which makes rattling noises when pulled. Baby cranes B and C are connected to the adult crane A at the wings; baby crane D is connected to baby cranes B and C. D is made up of two pieces of square papers folded together to make a single crane just as in #15 Yatsu hashi. In doing this, be sure to match white and black dots so that the wings are connected to each other.

Note:

You fold A first, then B, C, D in that order.

19. Saotome..... Girl Planting Rice

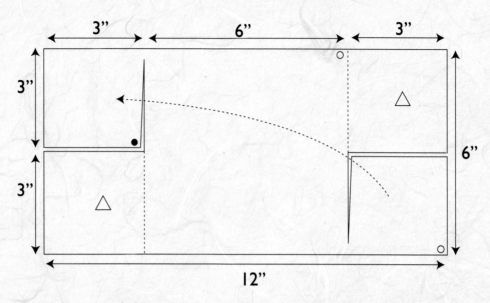

As in #18, Naruko, you fold two pieces of square paper together to make a single crane. Be sure to match the white and black dots. The baby crane looks like it is on a swing and is quite charming.

<u>Note:</u>

Fold the areas marked with triangles into the adult crane.

Remember to mark the heads and make all the creases before you fold.

Fold the adult crane first, then fold the baby crane, connecting its wings to the adult crane's wings.

20. Kanae..... Camping Stove

"Kanae" is an old Japanese word for a steel tripod. Three cranes are connected to make a tripod in this model.

Two square pieces (two C's) are folded together to make a single crane forming a circle.

Note:

Be sure to match white and black dots. Fold A and B first, then fold two C's.

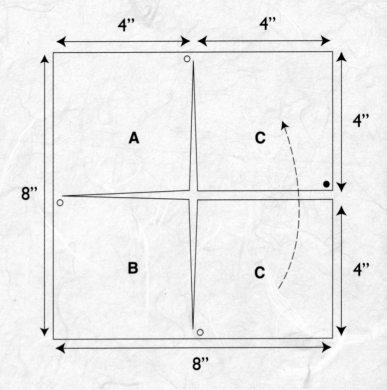

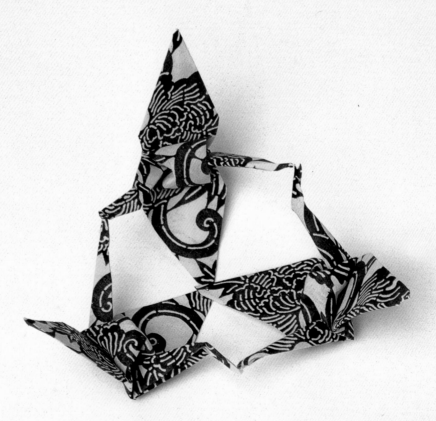

21. Kumanri..... Ninety Thousand Kilometers

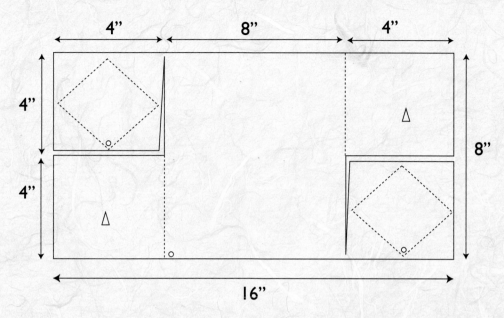

This model uses the "blintz fold". It is amazing that this designwhich resembles a jet was created 200 years ago.

Note:

Remember to make all the creases before you fold.

Remember to mark all the heads.

When you are doing a "blintz fold" it is very easy to lose the positions of the heads so pay extra attention to this.

22. Fuyo..... The Lotus Blossom

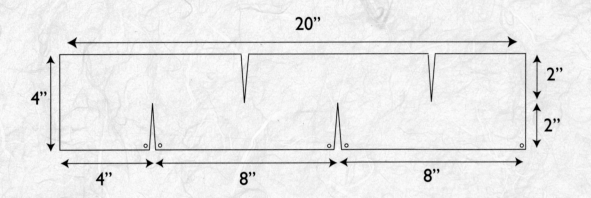

This is just like #4 Imoseyama, but it has more cranes. It looks easy, but it is very easy to lose the positions of the heads.

<u>Note:</u>

Remember to mark all the heads clearly and make all the creases before you fold. All the heads face the same direction. With the right kind of washi, this model could look just beautiful.

23. Hina Asobi..... Playing with Dolls

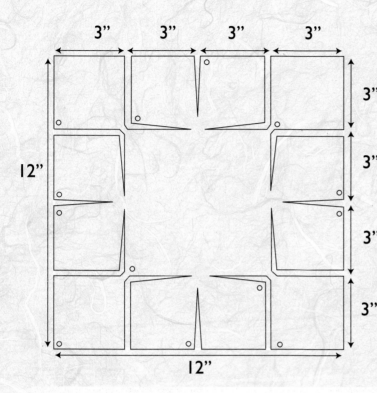

Four baby cranes are connected to the adult crane's head, tail, and both wings while eight more baby cranes are connected under the adult crane. In total there are twelve baby cranes connected to one adult crane. It is an impressive piece.

Note:
Remember to make all the creases and mark all the heads before you fold.
Fold the adult crane first.

24. Seikaiha..... Blue Ocean Wave

This resembles three #14 Inazuma models connected together. It is very beautiful but also very difficult, because the wings, heads and tails are all connected.

Note:

Start by folding one row at a time from the top following the A, B, C sequence.

Remember to make all the creases and mark all the heads before you fold.

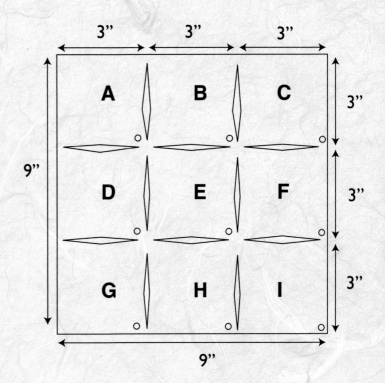

25. Tsuri Fune..... The Fishing Boat

This is big and beautiful but it is fairly easy to make. You use almost the whole sheet of washi.

Note:

Fold the adult crane first. Then you fold the baby cranes that are closest to the adult crane with a single paper up to the 5th crane. Then, from the 6th crane, you match and fold together square pieces from right and left to make a single crane. Square pieces are marked with alphabets. Match A to a, B to b, C to c and so on. When you match two square pieces, you put the wrong side of a paper to the wrong side of the other paper. Normally as in the other models where you put together two square pieces to fold a single crane, you would put the wrong side of a paper against the right side of a paper; but this is the only instance when it is not done that way. Remember to match white and black dots. The use of thin and strong washi, such as Jo-washi, is necessary.

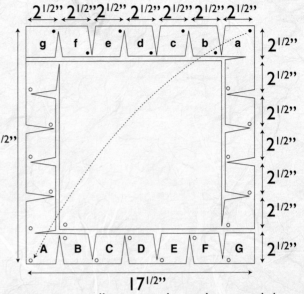

26. Mini-Noren..... Mini Room Divider
Created by Masako Sakai

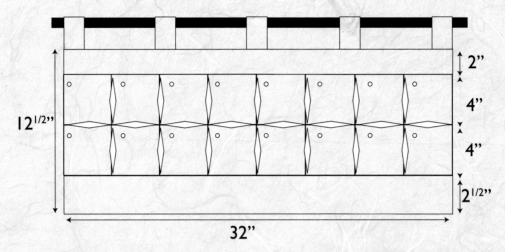

12 1/2"

2"

4"

4"

2 1/2"

32"

Noren is a room divider, but this is a smaller version that you can use as wall-hanging art. You would use half of the whole Ita jime washi. The whole Ita jime washi is approximately 25"x37". So you are using a sheet of washi which is 12.5"x37". After you cut the 12.5"x32" piece, you are left with a 12.5"x5" piece. You make straps out of this piece. You fold two rows of eight four-inch cranes all connected like #24 Seikaiha.

Note:

Remember to make all the creases and mark all the heads before folding. All the heads are facing in the same direction. After you fold all of the cranes, the folded area will become narrower than the unfolded area. Pleat the area above and below the folded area to match the width of the folded area. The straps for hanging the Noren are made out of five 1-1/2" x 3-1/2" strips of the same Ita jime washi. Put a bamboo stick through the straps and hang it on a wall.

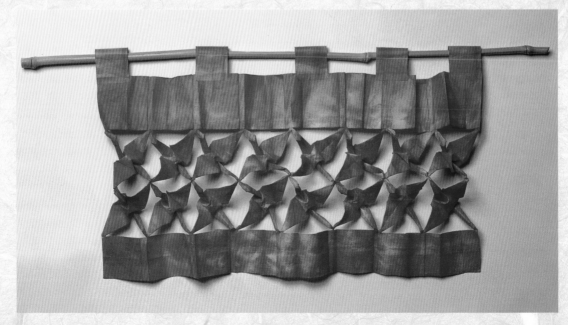

Part 3:

Presentation

Now that you have finished folding your origami, what do you do with it? Often it is left lying around or given to a friend who likes it but doesn't know what to do with it. Most people enjoy the process of folding and indeed with traditional origami made out of regular origami paper, you can simply enjoy the process of folding. With the Rokoan Origami Style however you should present the finished works nicely since you are using expensive washi and you have put so much time into folding. Show it off! Rokoan Origami is an art form.

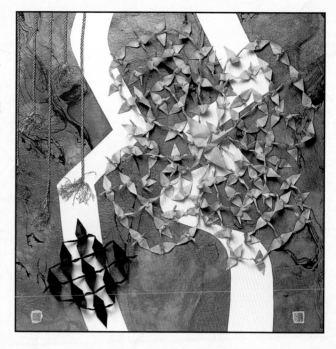

Just like any other work of art, the finished work should be presented to enhance enjoyment and appreciation as well as add value.

We are constantly looking for different display methods. Following are three of our suggestions.

Doll Cases

Plastic doll cases come in different sizes. We use 15cmx15cm (6"x6") and 12cmx12cm (4-³/₄"x4-³/₄") because they are not too big and not too small. Doll cases are good for most models. The models can be glued to the bottom, hung from the top or mounted on a stick that is glued to the bottom. We cover the bottom of the case with washi that is complimentary to the finished origami model to make a background for it. After securing your origami inside, you should cut the four walls of the case in accordance with the height of you origami. Then, after

placing the top, a ribbon or a metallic cord is tied to give a finishing touch. This is a great gift idea for weddings, birthdays or Christmas. Imoseyama made out of gorgeous red and gold washi in a case with gold cord is always an excellent wedding or anniversary gift.

Canvas Mount

For flat models like Inazuma, Seikaiha and Asagao, mounting on canvas is good. We use Premier canvas that is thick and does not have staples on the sides. You can paint or cover the background with washi, marbled paper or hand-made paper. Always remember to use a color that complements your origami. Use your imagination and have fun. When we glue down the origami, we like to be sure that the cranes are not too flat, but look alive and ready to fly. Once you have glued down the origami, the canvas piece is finsihed. If you want to keep it from being crushed, you can have it covered with Plexiglas.

Hanging Cranes

Origami cranes can be hung with a ribbon. They can be hung from a bamboo stick. Mini Noren is displayed this way. If you find a nice branch you can hang several origami such as Hina-asobi from it. Tsurifune is so magnificent that it can be hung by itself.